HOW TO STOP LIVING PAYCHECK TO PAYCHECK

Yes, You Can Be FINANCIALLY FREE!

Angelo Shamoon

www.Authorshub.ca
Facebook / Instagram: @authorshub.ca

Join the Movement!

Table of Contents

Special Thanks

Thank You!

Before beginning, I would like to say a special thanks to a few important people in my life who were instrumental to me writing this book.

The first would have to be my amazing wife of 9 years, Jackie, and her mom Laura. Without them, I would have never been able to conceive writing a book, let alone during the COVID-19 quarantine with 3 children all under the age of 7 years old! They both worked authentically hard to keep the distractions to a minimum and be a solid support system for me during this time. I am ever grateful for all you both have been able to accomplish with the home and the children while I was working on this book.

Secondly, I would like to thank YOU for purchasing this book. I am confident that, the contents of this book will reap great benefit, to those who read and apply the lessons and recommendations, in the best way possible, to their financial situation.

Please don't forget to leave your positive review aswell.

Let's jump in!

Introduction

Financial freedom, at last, does not equal being a millionaire or even rich. It means that you are not enslaved anymore by credit or money. You can walk pretty much anywhere and buy whatever you want within your means by just signing for it. Some would-be buyers are not even asked any proof of income, pay stubs, etc. simply because they have perfect or near-perfect credit.

Lenders know that this person makes good on his promise to pay for things. This person is either not afraid to work for money or somehow was blessed with a good retirement, made good money and can manage it or inherited it, but didn't squander it away. This all means this person is responsible for his management of money and can be trusted. Those who line the supermarket isles making a long line to buy the lotto at least have a dream of becoming millionaires and ending the financial noose around their neck. But even if they're lucky enough to win the millions, will they be financially free? How many cases have you heard of people who have won the Lotto, squandered it all and wound up worse off than ever? Actually, from what I've read or heard, it's most lotto winners.

Sure, it's very nice to have millions in the bank and not have to worry about having to get up every day and go to work. Many sudden new millionaires, such as lottery winners take off right away, leaving their jobs, friends, and acquaintances behind. But after a year, maybe two, they begin to miss what they had. Even the "burden" of work doesn't seem as bad anymore. Many retirees become "free" of financial stress with their retirement money and die not long after retiring. I know many who simply refuse to retire because they know the end would come soon.

Remember that to be truly financially free you will require putting energy into it. Money is condensed energy. No. I don't mean work 15 hours a day till you drop. But oddly enough work keeps you happy and motivated and your morale high. The more creative you are with work, the better the ideas that you put to use and the more your product is in demand and people are willing to buy it from you, the more money you will have. Those who have trouble with even the thought of expending energy to work are financial slaves and resort to violations of how money is earned. Enjoy work, enjoy working for the sake of being productive and you'll never be a slave to money, for you'll always have more than enough than you need and you'll be financially free.

So, financial freedom has two sides to it. It doesn't belong to the non-industrious and the avoiders of work. It is not for those Wall street types with the golden parachutes. It belongs to those who value credit and value money enough to continue to honestly and industriously make it, for they never have to worry. They can always make more. For them, the financial world depends on how they keep spinning. They are truly financially free.

Understanding Financial Freedom

It is important to a lot of people or a vast majority of people that they can satisfy their needs or desires at whatever time it arises. However, many are not equipped with the mentality to actualize this desire; hence, the need for financial freedom. The meaning of financial freedom is subjective to different people and the various situation they find themselves. For a teenager, financial freedom is independence from parents; it is them not having to depend on the income or allowances given by the parents. Therefore, teenagers might regard themselves financially free if they have their income which funds their lifestyle irrespective of the benefits provided by the parents. To a retiree, it is the freedom to have the desired lifestyle without the stress of bankruptcy because of the retirement plans or investments that have been set in place. To some people, it the ability to perform in a role they admire or remain self-employed without strain on their finances.

However, financial freedom, in general, refers to a lifestyle void of the concern or domination of income. In clear terms, it refers to the ability or status of a person to provide or support a need in whatever circumstance. It is a position where you are settled financially; any unplanned or sudden expense will not cause a dent to your financial state. It refers to a state of being economically independent without having to depend on salaries from employment. It is also important to note that financial freedom connotes a debt-free situation; that is; a person who wants to lay claim that he is financially free cannot claim that the money that funds his free state is from debt. Financial freedom is not restricted to being able to only fund emergencies but also to find solace in the fact that your life after retirement has specific plans in place that would ensure financial stability and growth. It's not a lifestyle that is dominated by money and a constant worry to make the money.

It also entails the ability to retire early or quit a job simply because you have lost interest in that particular field but do not have a specific task that you are registered to at that specific time. It is the ability to afford a desired lifestyle without stress about the next paycheck. Therefore, you are in control of your finance and lifestyle instead of your financial state dictating a particular lifestyle it believes you can afford without collapse. It is the ability to work for cooperation or company based on the fact that you enjoy whatever role you are given and not because it is crucial to your finance.

Financial Independence?

"Financial independence is the fiscal status of a person or family that meets the necessities of money related opportunity with two or three varieties. The ultimate goal for a person or family who strives to be financially independent is to have the option of retiring earlier or continuing to work (on their terms).

Covered debt:

If used with care, covered debt can be used to finance investments that can help create wealth. This means that you are using debt as leverage to finance an investment that is secured by an asset. A popular case of covered debt is the mortgage for rental property. The mortgage is the debt. Property is the asset that "covers" the debt. In other words, if the property were sold, you would pay the mortgage in full. Covered debt is not necessary to meet the conditions of financial independence but is often used to obtain it.

Retirement savings:

Strive to save enough for the traditional retirement period so you don't have to rely on supplementary social security income or a pension. Income from social security or a pension is just the icing on the cake. Maximizing tax-advantaged accounts may or may not be the best strategy for everyone, but generally, it is. Savers who maximize their accounts with tax advantages generally do so to defer/avoid taxes or for succession/heritage purposes.

Investment Income:

Those seeking to be financially independent generally have a significant portion of their investments in taxable accounts. One technique is to have enough savings in taxable accounts to accommodate a retirement rate that will last until the period in which you can begin withdrawing your retirement savings. Then withdrawals would begin from retirement accounts to the end of life. Another strategy is to have enough in taxable accounts where investment income would cover all expenses for life (including travel and fun things), thus allowing minimal withdrawals from tax-advantaged accounts later in life. Cash flow from investments replaces earned income, freeing you from relying on others for a living.

What's the Difference?

There's not much difference. Financial freedom means you have no debts and are financially stable. You are prepared to deal with what life throws at you without the worry of living from one paycheck to another. You're working, enjoying life, and preparing for a comfortable retirement. However, financial independence brings you to a whole different level. You're the epitome of living below your means. You're saving all you can and you're investing or running your own business. You'll retire early, do whatever you want, and you'll have to explain yourself to no one.

Importance of Financial Freedom

It is the case that some people are not concerned about financial freedom, they are satisfied with the lifestyle of dependence on salaries and working for corporations because of their financial state, they are not concerned with the profits and interest from investing. However, apart from the benefits and advantages of financial independence, it also gives you the plan to schedule your day or time according to your desire. Your life is fixed with things that sincerely interest you. Therefore, you have the freedom of choice to select any of the following options;

There is no compulsion to work with or for a company, a financially free person has enough funds to identify a hobby as a job daily even though it might not provide as much as an actual job. The liberty to work based on the fact that you enjoy something rather than the necessity to fund your lifestyle. It puts you in a relaxed and settled position or situation to do whatever you want. For instance, a financially free person who does not work for a company has the liberty and the funds to travel anywhere at any time without any impact on his status. However, someone else would have to apply for a break at their corporation to attend to this. You have the liberty to plan your schedule and work at any time you desire. Financial Freedom does not only include being able to support your desired lifestyle. It also entails being able to assist and fund those who need this help.

Mentality for Financial Freedom Success

The number one thing you can do for yourself when it comes to establishing a strong foundation to begin to build your success is to check your mentality and prime your mindset. Your mind is the strongest tool you have, and it offers you the biggest advantage when it comes to achieving anything you want in this lifetime. If you learn how to understand your mind and use it to your advantage, you will always have the upper hand in every area of your life because you will be equipped with the strongest tool there is. There is absolutely nothing in this world that has not been accomplished by a strong mind; every single progression and achievement humankind has made has been driven by someone who knew how to activate and harness the power of their mind. If you want to achieve great things in this lifetime, you need to learn how to activate and harness that very same power.

Your mindset is and always will be the number one difference you have from the people around you, and it is something that will stay with you no matter what. While other things could fall apart or unexpected problems may arise, your mindset will always keep you moving forward. That is because of how powerful it is; thus, you must master your mind before you move on to developing your personal and professional plans. Doing this beforehand ensures that your dreams are truly personal to you and that they offer you what you truly want in this lifetime. This way, you do not develop dreams based on someone else's desires or someone else's beliefs.

Another big reason behind why you want to develop your mindset early on is that it will support you with creating an incredibly powerful plan that has the potential to take you where you want to go. If you do not take the time to master your mindset first, your plan may be ridden with weaknesses and downfalls that prevent it from being strong enough to help you discover your desired results. To make sure that your foundation is truly as strong as it needs to be, we are going to start by identifying what mentality you need to have and what perspectives you need to foster to help you succeed.

The Trailblazer Mentality

When it comes to cultivating success in your life, you need to start by having a leadership mentality. The leadership mentality does not necessarily mean that you are going to lead other people, although many people with the leadership mentality do step into the role of leaders and happily take these roles on in their lives. What the leadership mentality does mean is that you are going to take on the role of being a leader in your own life so that you can lead yourself to the greatness and success that you desire. The leadership mentality is something that we create, not something we are gifted with. Every single leader you see and that you may admire right now has spent time learning how to become a leader by nurturing their mindset and discovering the mentality that comes with being a leader. As they continue to educate themselves on and acknowledge this practice, they find themselves becoming better and better at leading themselves and, consequently, at leading others, too.

The mindset of a leader is characterized by many different things, but there are generally seven key characteristics that absolutely every single leader must have to be successful in their lives. These characteristics include openness, ambition, a desire for ROI (Return On Investment), belief that it is important, fear of the consequences of inaction, self-knowing, and a commitment to self-improvement. If you can develop and work on these seven characteristics in your life, you can develop your role as being a leader in your life so that you can lead yourself to greatness. Openness or open-mindedness is important because it provides you with the opportunity to always remain willing to see beyond your current perspective. Leaders know that they are not the only ones privy to good ideas or good information, and they know that the way to get their hands on more good ideas and good information is to remain open. As such, they are always focused on maintaining an open mind and keeping themselves as receptive to new ideas and new possibilities as they can.

Leaders remain ambitious in that they are always open for improvement and they are always trying to advance themselves in as many different ways as they possibly can. They are hungry for opportunity, growth, and advancement and so they are always focused on moving forward in as many ways as they can. Often, a truly powerful leader is growing in many ways at any given time because they know they have the energy and potential to do so much more than anyone thing in their lives. If you do find yourself leading a team, you should also be focused on developing ambition in your team as well so that as you lead them you are also supporting them in becoming leaders in their own lives, too. A desire for ROI essentially means that a leader is always willing to work hard but they must know that there is going to be a reasonable payoff for the work that they are doing. Leaders are not just interested in small ROI's, either. They want to know that they are getting the absolute biggest payoff from their investment possible to ensure that they are investing in the smartest ways they can.

This includes utilizing time, energy, money, knowledge, effort, and anything else they might invest in something. Because of that fact, if a leader invests in you, you should know that it is because they see potential in you and they believe that you are going to have a high "payoff" in the long run. In addition to knowing that they will get a high ROI, a leader also needs to know that what they are investing in is important. True leaders will never invest in something if they cannot see the importance of it because, no matter how much they may get in return, it seems pointless if there is no real value behind what they are investing in. Leaders are often committed to at least one major cause or purpose in their lifetimes that keeps them moving forward and creating whatever it is they believe holds enough value to be worth their investment. In a sense, this is the long-game ROI where they are investing their ultimate amount of time, energy, money, knowledge, and effort into one major overall thing that they hope will have a huge payoff in the long run.

Aside from being highly driven toward something, leaders are also highly driven away from something, too. They are driven away through the fear of what the consequences might be if they never take action on something. They are afraid that if they don't act, the consequences will be much higher than the risk of taking action, and so leaders will always act despite risk because they know it is better than sitting around wishing they had tried. Of course, they will always do what they can to minimize the risk, but they will still move forward despite any risks that may exist so that they can enjoy the possible benefits of the action they took should its payoff in the long run.

Self-knowing is something that often seems surprising to people who have not yet dug into their leadership style, yet it is highly important in regards to becoming a leader. Self-knowing allows people to continually learn more about themselves and what they truly care about or what they want to accomplish in the world. Often, you will hear about leaders going on some sort of journey or trip that resulted in them doing soul-searching and learning extremely intimate and important facts about themselves along the way. This process of getting to know yourself and learning to deeply understand who you are and what drives you is what allows you to better understand how you can lead yourself and how you can lead others.

In addition to self-knowing, a leader should also always remain committed to self-improvement. Self-improvement is how you take the findings from what you have learned about yourself and turn them into something that results in you evolving and becoming even better over time. Through self-improvement, you can offset any flaws or faults you may have and launch yourself toward greatness by regularly pushing for better and better. Through this, your results grow massively and you can continually move forward in life. Only fellow leaders will understand why consistent growth matters, as it seems like anyone who is not a leader seems perfectly fine remaining stagnant in the same comfortable conditions all of their life. To a leader, especially one that has taken the time to develop their leadership qualities, remaining stagnant and comfortable is possibly one of the worst things they could ever experience. They crave growth, even if they cannot always explain why.

The Art of Always Learning

Entrepreneurs and leaders have one massive thing in common and it is that they are always learning. To always be learning means to have a growth mindset, and a growth mindset is indicative of a successful leader and entrepreneur. With your growth mindset, you can see the world as a place that is abundant with opportunity and potential and as a place where you can exist to learn from those opportunities and that potential. You discover ways that you can become even better, and you find opportunities to always grow within yourself and within the world around you.

When you have a growth mindset, you believe that all of your abilities and skills can be improved upon and you believe that you have the potential to do so. This means that you are always open to the possibility that even things that come hard to you right now can be improved so that you can do better and they can become easier for you in the future. With a real growth mindset, the belief does not extend just in any one area of your life, but rather in all areas of your life. People with a growth mindset genuinely believe that they can improve upon anything they want to and that if they are willing to put the energy in, they can develop skills in any given area of their lives.

Having a growth mindset is important, and you should strive to develop your growth mindset within yourself. In doing so, you keep yourself open to the potential and ability to learn more as you go, which means that you will always have access to the knowledge that you need to get the outcomes you wish. This essentially leads to you having an open mind, but in a way, that means you are not only willing to learn more but you are also willing to try more. Which is, in fact, another key difference between leaders and non-leaders.

Being willing to learn more is great, but you should also be willing to implement any new knowledge or lessons that you come across along the way. To be able to do this, you first need to be able to decern which lessons or skills are worth learning, and which are not going to be worth your time. This is where it is helpful to be able to use a need for a high ROI and a need for what you are doing to be important. If you can identify the high ROI from the lesson or practice and you can recognize its importance, you have a lesson or practice that is well worth the effort for you to give it a try.

After you have decided to try something new, you also need to be willing to monitor that new thing as you go. You need to implement it thoroughly and to the best of your ability, while also monitoring it to make sure that it is giving you the results you desire. If you find it is not, don't give up! You can pivot and try to adapt your approach to improve your ability to get the results you desire. If after a few attempts and pivots, however, you find that it is not giving you the results you need and you cannot see how it possibly could – be willing to peacefully let go of that practice and move onto something likely to give you a better payoff.

Knowing the difference between what is a good idea and what is not, and what is working and what is not, is incredibly important when you are trying to develop as a person. In being able to decern this type of information you allow yourself to make sure that you are always trying new things but that you are never wasting your time on any practices that are not serving you. The real key here is knowing how long to put your effort in, as you do not want to give up before you have a chance to get results, but you also do not want to hold onto something that is not going to give you results in the first place. You can find that sweet spot through regularly reviewing new practices and even working with mentors on them to make sure that you are using them properly before giving upon them.

The Planner Mindset

When it comes to planning, I want you to focus on the mindset you foster. Having the right mindset with planning is important as it ensures that you are going to approach your entire planning process in an effective manner that leads to you getting the results you desire. Since the rest of this book is largely focused on planning and executing plans, you can see why this is an incredibly important mindset for you to understand and implement in your life.

The thing about planning that most people do not realize is that plans are a much stronger tool than people often give them credit for. Having strong, well-developed plans is the key to having success in anything in your life, and knowing how to rely on those plans and follow them through is important, too. Ideally, you want to see your plans as being the foundation for absolutely everything going forward, and as with any foundation, you need that foundation to be as strong as possible to make sure it can handle everything you are building on it. If you do not take the time to build your plans to be a strong and powerful foundation, then chances are you are not going to be able to build anything significant off of your plans.

When it comes to approaching your plans, you need to respect them for being the strong foundation they are meant to be. This means you need to be ready to immediately start by not only developing plans but refining those plans and researching everything you need to make sure that those plans are as strong as they possibly can be. When you have completed your plans, you should feel confident that everything you have put in them is thoroughly researched and is true to the best of your ability so that when it comes time to follow those plans you can follow them without having to think about them. This way, rather than wasting time wondering if the plan is strong enough or trying to refine your plan along the way you can invest all of your time and energy into seeing that plan through and making it work for you. As a result, you are far more likely to make results from your plan because you will have made one that was designed to get you the results you desire.

One thing you need to be particularly careful about when it comes to planning is making sure that you have planned well enough but that you are not finding yourself stuck in analysis paralysis when it comes to your plan. If you find yourself planning too long, you may just turn the planning phase into an excuse to procrastinate rather than using it as a tool to help you create the results you desire. Be watchful of this!

The sweet spot is spending enough time on your plan that you feel confident in it and accepting the fact that it will never be perfect and that if you need to you can adapt it at any point in the future to help you get the results you desire. If you do find yourself succumbing to analysis paralysis you might just find that you benefit from scheduling a few "reviews" into your plan so that you know when you can review your plan to see how you are doing.

Knowing that these reviews are in the future may just give you the motivation you need to move past analysis and planning and into the process of actually starting to implement your plan and move forward in achieving the results you desire. While planning is largely something that has a clear and easy-to-follow beginning, middle, and ending to it, it can help to adapt planning techniques and styles that may make planning even easier for you. The more you can adapt your planning strategies to suit your needs, while still upholding the primary purpose and benefit of planning, the better you will become at planning and the stronger your plans will become, too.

Stop Living Paycheck to Paycheck

Learn to Manage Your Money

To begin our journey to financial freedom with the opportunities presented to us online. First, we will have to begin to manage our money, this will be a difficult decision because, to achieve the objective we set ourselves, we have to change our way of thinking and being, we have to know how much money we are earning in our work and how much we are losing in daily expenses. We have to make a record of our expenses: car, house, telephone, television, and others. The first thing we should do is stop using our credit cards, stop acquiring debt, and start living to the fullest. An example of this is that if we decide to buy a television and the price of this one on credit is worth 30% more than the price of the same equipment in debit but it allows you to pay it little by little, this is a debt that makes your monthly money more difficult for you to save it because you will always be charged monthly for a certain time and the interest charged by banks on credit cards continues to grow.

That's why you have to focus on reducing your expenses, you have to start saving your money. Offer to save 10% of your monthly income, create a bank account and if you can configure this account to give you a discount of 10% of your monthly money, so you will stop seeing that money that is not in your account, if not that this money goes directly to your other savings account. You have to learn to say No when you need to buy something, and you don't have the money in your account but remember that you have money saved and you could use it to buy what you want. You have to think that you are collecting money to get your financial freedom and if you start touching that money you have been saving for some time, you will not be able to leave the place where you are, so you must say No.

When you are invited to a bar or a restaurant, think about how that will help you change your economic situation; if it happens to presents a chance to change you can go but if the answer is no, you have to say no. You have to change the way you are living and if it is necessary to change the people around you, do it, you have to know people who think about a better future, who think about making money and not only think about it but who are always looking for the way forward, looking for information about the market, thinking about how to change the economic situation or as the millionaires would say: You have to surround yourself with masterminds. This will help you understand that changing your attitude is easier to learn how to save money and where to spend it.

After this, we will begin to invest in ourselves. You have to decide what you want, how much money you need to live as you want, what you have to learn and how to learn, how much time you got to apply to attain whatever you want. You have to create an image of yourself in the future, how you would like things to be. You have to start taking care of yourself through preparation. Before starting to invest, we have to organize our lives, our expenses, and our income to move in the right direction, to achieve the goals we have set for ourselves.

In summary, to manage your money you can follow this series of steps:
1.- Record your expenses. This is the first step to saving your money, you need to know how much you are spending for a month.
Make a budget: After recording your monthly expenses, you can organize a budget of what you can spend monthly and what you can save.
3.- Plan your money-saving: Taking into account monthly expenses and income, create a savings portfolio where you have to deliver a minimum of 10% of your monthly income.
Establish objectives: Taking into account your monthly income, propose quarterly or half-yearly objectives that give you an idea of how much you have to save to reach those objectives. After the COVID-19 pandemic, I'm sure we have all come to learn what non-essential items can be removed from our monthly expenses and live without. Direct that income towards your savings portfolio! There is no excuse for not being able to come up with that 10% to put aside!!!
5.- Have priorities: Each person has priorities, according to this is that they decide to save money, find your priorities, and focus your savings plans on it.
6.- Save money with automatic transfers: Choose how often you want to transfer money from your primary account to your savings account.

7.- Watch your savings grow: Monitor the progress of your monthly savings, this will help you improve the ways you can achieve your goals. Here's a passage that I liked a lot and I think it is the basis for everyone who wants to start creating their wealth.

"Wealth, like a tree, is born of a seed. The first coin you save will be the seed of the tree that will make your wealth grow." George Clason.

Learn how to manage your time.

Part of the whole world of online investment depends on the information you manage, that's why you must learn to manage the time you have to look for information about the stock market and the different companies that are in this place. You have to know how to schedule your free time, you have a family and you want to spend time with them, but you also worry about the expenses you have to give them and the life they want. That's why we have to find a space to learn about the different ways in which you can earn extra money from home, because the more information you have, it will be easier to know where you can invest your money and your time to achieve what many already have financial freedom. The time you have to learn will give you the necessary tools to know everything about the different instruments that exist to create wealth. Some tips that might help you get started maybe:

Don't spend your time on things you can't control, concentrate on the things you can do and how to do them to get what you need, always think if what you're about to do is going to give you something you're looking for, if the answer is no, then change and find another way. Remember—ROI!

Do not expect results immediately, this is always a problem because many of those who start in this, want to be rewarded for their effort immediately, when the truth is that this is a world where profits are reflected as time goes by, everything starts slow and grows slowly. So, don't despair and be patient, things will come in their time, just keep focused on what you want to achieve.

Don't give up for failing the first time, no one has ever succeeded in their first attempt. You always have to keep trying and at some point, you will, that's why patience and time are important factors in creating income.

Don't let others influence your emotions and discourage you by seeing that you can't earn extra income, remember that you're the one who's trying without giving up because you know it's just a matter of time before you get what you're looking for. Remember that you are trying while those people who want to influence you to quit don't even dare to try for fear of failure. These are the so-called "Naysayers". These Naysayers are almost always over conservative and critically negative and you know who they are – STAY AWAY from these types of people. If it is impossible to stay away from someone like this because they are a family member or an individual that you must cross paths within an ongoing basis, then avoid disclosing your plans, hopes and dreams to them. They are still people you can love and befriend, but maybe not the best person to help feed your motivation to accomplish your dreams. Until when? For some it's forever; they will just have to be spectator/s (some of us have more than one in our life) of your results and watch your milestones as they come, for others, it could be wisest to share as your results come! This way it leaves no room for negativity, but a celebration for what has been accomplished each time instead. You will just need to decern which person fits in which category and live your life by fulfilling your plans, aiming for results. Go ahead and don't let anyone discourage you.

Here are some tips you can implement to help you make the most of your time:

1. Leave aside perfectionism and seek to produce good results.
2. Organize your activities. Keep in mind the tasks you have to do each day and organize everything so you can make the most of your time.
3. Perform a cleaning: Change the work area where you develop, clean everything both physically and mentally and you will be able to focus better on your goals.

Find out what skills and abilities you possess so that you can develop better and focus your energy on that.

Steps to Suitably Manage Your Money to Financial Freedom

Before you move forward with the professional and entrepreneurial aspects of your plan, I want to discuss the important topic of managing your money. Every single person should take time in their lives to learn about important money management skills and, if you are in the process of building your own business, you need to do it soon rather than later. The sooner you can develop the skills to manage your own money effectively, the easier it will be for you to manage your money and the money belonging to the business that you are building your wealth through.

There are two elements to managing money that everyone needs to know about: what to do with the money, and how to get the most out of the money you have. Knowing where to put your money, how to use your money, and what to expect from your money is an important step when it comes to wealth management because it allows you to know that your money is working for you. This way, not only do you have some saved but you also have some of your money developing more money through the form of investments, meaning your money is effectively protecting you against things like losses or inflation. You also need to know how to get the most out of the money you have because, to put it frankly, no truly successful entrepreneur has ever let a lack of finances hold them back from achieving their success.

Many massive entrepreneurs from Jeff Bezos to Steve Jobs were largely broke when they started their businesses, and yet through effective use of their money, they were able to get their businesses going and develop massive funds as a result. Knowing what to do with the money you have right now, and then what to do with the wealth you develop will go a long way in helping you have strong experience with your money. This way, you do not find yourself mismanaging your money and ending up broke in the long run, or ultimately bankrupting your plan due to financial mistakes that could have easily been avoided.

Plan for Your Future

In addition to having an emergency fund that can be accessed at any time, you should also have funds that are being set aside for your future. Setting funds aside for your future ensures that you will have enough money to retire and do whatever you want for the rest of your life. When it comes to setting funds aside for your future, you should be focused on setting aside at least 10-15% of your funds for retirement specifically. These funds can be invested in any form of investment that is going to protect your assets while also giving you a decent return on your investment. Some organizations have investment products you can place your retirement money into; that results in you earning a matched amount on your investment up to a certain amount, meaning that for every $1 you invest you are given back $1 and it earns interest. Having these types of funds opened and otherwise investing in portfolios that are going to give you a strong return is a great idea as it ensures that your money is growing while it waits for you to retire. This way, you have far more than you ever invested and you are protected against things like inflation.

It is important to understand that once your debt is paid off and you have accumulated more wealth, you will want to take an additional percentage and invest it into things like higher risk investment portfolios. However, your retirement funds should always stay in either low or moderate risk investments to ensure that you are never risking your future. Let the other funds you invest take the risk and possibly earn you massive results, instead. That way, you are investing wisely and you have the potential to earn more without the risk of losing everything you have.

Monitor Your Credit

Assuming credit companies will monitor your credit and protect you against mistakes or flaws is a bad idea, and assuming that simply paying your debt off will give you a strong enough credit rating is also a bad idea. You need to regularly monitor your credit scores and pay attention to how your credit report reads so that you understand what is affecting your credit and what you can do to protect yourself against that.

The best way to maintain your credit is to pay your debt off, then keep your credit cards at 25% or less of their total capacity. For example, only carry a $250 balance on a $1,000 credit limit. This number is the sweet spot for a strong credit rating and will ensure that you never get yourself into a position that you cannot reasonably manage.

In addition to keeping your credit low, also make sure that you are incredibly honest with yourself about what type of debt you can handle going forward. Buying vehicles with a loan or taking out a mortgage, for example, is not a bad idea, so long as you can handle it. Do not assume that just because you pass the credit score means that you can handle the debt that you are looking at taking on because in most cases it does not. Instead, look at your actual budget and see how much you can reasonably afford to put toward things like car loans and mortgages, to be confident in the debt you decide to take on.

Remove Unnecessary Expenses

In addition to paying off debts, you need to start removing unnecessary expenses from your budget. Unnecessary expenses are any expenses that you are paying for things that you are not using or things that you are not getting enough value out of. Removing unnecessary expenses ensures that you are freeing up more of your finances to put toward things that matter, and it also helps you with cleaning up your budget overall. Don't wait for something horrible to occur to you in life to see the importance of this. This is one of a few other reasons COVID-19 was a blessing. For the majority, COVID-19 forced us to cut expenses and relearn what the difference between needs and wants is. Some who were living on a monthly expense of $6,000/month learned that, by reducing non-essential expenses from their overall budget, they reduced their monthly expenses substantially by a couple thousand. True story!!

If you cannot eliminate certain expenses, consider cutting them down to as low as they can be so that you are not spending any unnecessary money on things that you should not be spending money on. For example, lower your cell phone plan or your internet or cable plan to make sure that you are not spending any unnecessary money. If you have streaming services or subscription services, make sure you pay for only the specific level of each subscription you need. It might appear to be perfect to get "the best," particularly if the cost distinction between a littler membership and a bigger membership is certifiably not a major bounce, yet the truth is that if you are not using the bigger subscription, it is a waste of your money. While $5 per subscription may not seem like a lot if you are paying for more than you need on just 4 subscriptions, that is $20 a month or $240 a year. While $240 may not seem like a lot, that may be an entire week of groceries or extra funds placed into an investment. If you are running a business, $240 may even be enough to cover an entire years' worth of website hosting or another similar service that benefits your business and earns you money. When it comes to wealth development, no amount of money is insignificant, no matter how seemingly small it may be.

Keep an Emergency Fund

One of the first budget goals you should have for yourself is developing an emergency fund. Ideally, you should be developing your emergency fund alongside paying off debt as being your two number one priorities if you are new to wealth management. Emergency funds are necessary as they prevent you from dipping into debt pools to pay for emergencies that you may happen upon and, the reality is, there will always be unexpected expenses that you have to pay for. Keeping a reasonable reserve of funds available ensures that you can pay for unnecessary expenses out of pocket so that you are not going into debt over those expenses.

The size emergency fund you will need ultimately depends on who you are and what your lifestyle is like. However, it is generally recommended that you have an emergency fund of at least 3-6 months' worth of your income available to ensure that if anything ever went wrong you would be supported. For the average family, this means you should have about $30,000 aside in a savings account for your emergency fund. Of course, this may seem overwhelming or intimidating at first, but you do not have to put this money aside immediately. You can start by putting aside one months' salary, and then moving on to paying off your debt. Once your debt is paid off, however, you should make it a priority to get 3-6 months' salary aside as soon as possible. Another simple and practical way to accumulate your emergency fund to where it needs to be is by following the 80/20 rule. Set aside 20% of your entire income for yourself. 10% of that goes to your savings portfolio, the other 10% goes toward your emergency fund. The remaining 80% will be dedicated to your monthly living expenses. If you want a strong savings account, you should be focused on getting that number up to 6-12 months' salary so that you can handle any unexpected expense that might come your way, including a job loss.

Your emergency fund should be something that is always kept as a liquid asset that is not tied up into any sort of term investment. Because of the nature of these funds you need to feel confident that you are going to be able to access them at a moments' notice without any concern. If you were to have those funds tied up in assets or term investments, accessing it could cost you some hefty fees and that would completely defy the entire purpose of those funds.

Have A Budget

A budget may be one of the most basic wealth management tools a person can use, and yet many people overlook the idea of budgeting and instead attempt to manage their wealth spontaneously. This is not effective in helping you create the long-term wealth you desire because it results in money being mismanaged, misused, and misplaced. Often, people without budgets find themselves spending money they should not have, carrying unnecessary expenses, and failing to save any money because they have no idea what they can save. Rather than having any long-term success, they end up draining their financial assets every time they come upon them and, as a result, find themselves struggling in the long run. Save yourself some pain and take Benjamin Franklin's advice "If you fail to plan, you are planning to fail!".

Creating a budget is not difficult and allows you to know exactly where your money is going and what you are doing with your money. Ideally, you should have budgets planned out for 3, 6, and 12-month intervals. Your 3-month budgets should be extremely detailed with your earnings and expenses are all written out to the dollar. Your six- and twelve-month budgets can be projections of what you anticipate you will have and what you anticipate you will be able to do with that money. Having all of these budgets created ensures that you have a clear understanding as to what you are working toward so that you can always make financial choices that are *on track* with your long-term financial plans and goals. After you have these longer goals in place, you should focus on reviewing your budget every month, as well as every single time you receive money whether it is expected or unexpected. This way, you can ensure that your budget accurately reflects all the funds you have and makes the most out of the money that you have earned.

Understand Your Expenses

Through creating your budget, you will realize that you have many expenses you need to account for and consider on a monthly and yearly basis. Understanding what your expenses are and how they are affecting you is important as it allows you to know exactly what you are spending your money on and why. You would be surprised how many people do not know what their expenses are or how much they owe monthly, and as a result, they find themselves missing payments and having services shut off because they mismanaged their funds.

Keeping track of all of your expenses is incredibly easy, but it is also incredibly important. You can do so by going through all of your statements and identifying every single expense you are paying on a month to month basis and writing it down on your "master budget" list. This budget list should allow you to see exactly what it is that you are spending your money on so that you understand where your money is going and why it is going there.

It is extremely important that when you start tracking your expenses, you track more than just your mandatory bills. You should also track your leisurely spending habits and any other spending habits you might have to make sure that you are getting an accurate representation of where your money is going. This is going to help you when it comes to shaping your budget by allowing you to see where you may be overspending, as well as what types of spending are most important to you.

Understand Your Income

In addition to acknowledging your expenses, you also need to acknowledge your income. You likely know exactly what it is that you get paid monthly, but you want to make sure you keep track of this number so that you can incorporate it into your budget. You also want to be aware of any additional funds you may receive, such as any form of expected or unexpected money that you receive from outside of your salary. Most people view this money as being "extra" and will happily spend it on things like extra clothes, extra visits to a restaurant, or any other leisurely expenses. If you are setting yourself up to build and maintain wealth, though, you are going to want to stop seeing this as being extra and start seeing this as being a part of your overall income. Then, you should incorporate it into your budget and use it *wisely*.

While applying some of your extra funds toward leisurely purchases is a great idea, you should refrain from placing all of your extra funds toward leisurely purchases. The reality is, your leisurely purchases are likely not as big of a priority to you as your budget goals are; however, at the moment, they may feel like a great idea. It is easy to experience impulses around money, especially impulses that bring about instant gratification. However, this instant gratification is often the number one thing that leads to people experiencing buyer's remorse and can even lead to or reinforce poor spending habits. The more *intentional* you are, the more effective you will be with your money. Always focus on building stronger spending habits, even in areas where it seems harmless or like it should just be a "one-time thing." The more intentional you are, the more impactful you will be with your finances.

Pay Off Your Debt

Debt is something that can be leveraged and used in an incredibly positive and powerful way if it is used properly. However, most people carry their debt as a burden and fail to make the most out of it and as a result find themselves struggling to manage their debt. In many cases, this also leads to poor credit ratings which can harm your financial outlook in the future.

If you want to start making stronger financial moves and using your money in a way that improves your life and the business you will be growing, you need to pay off your debt and then begin managing your debt properly. Ideally, you should pay off your debt as quickly as you can and as effectively as you can. Most wealth management advisors will suggest paying off all unnecessary debt first before even considering a savings account because your money will be costing you more on a credit card than it will earn you in a savings account. By paying off your debt you save massive amounts of money every month which means that you will be able to put even more away or use it for other important things such as business expenses.

After you have paid off your debt, you do not want to be afraid to develop new debt. However, you do need to be vigilant to make sure that you are using your debt properly and not burying yourself under debt that you may or may not be able to handle. Make sure that your debt is always manageable, and that you are only accumulating debt over things that are worth going into debt over. As well, always have a plan to pay off your debt before you get into debt so that your credit rating stays strong and your finances stay healthy. Often, there are debt classes you can take in most cities that will support you in understanding how debt works and how to use it, but you can also talk to a bank advisor if you are not entirely sure. The more you can educate yourself on this topic, however, the more likely you will be to use your debt to your advantage rather than feeling as though you are burying yourself under a mountain that you can't dig yourself out from under.

Invest Where It Matters

As you go on in life, and especially if you plan on starting a business, you need to make sure that you always invest when and where it matters. Knowing how to prioritize your expenses and spend your money on what truly matters ensures that you will always have exactly what you need to move forward to the next step. Investing in exactly what you need does not mean that you will not get everything else, it simply means you are investing in exactly what you need to *create* the funds for everything else you want in life.

The best way to see where you really should be investing your money is to look at your long-term plan and honestly identify where you need to invest your money. Make sure that you start by spending your money on what is going to get you the furthest. For example: if you are starting with an e-commerce business, invest $300 into a basic laptop, $150 into a self-managed and self-designed website, $50 into a good payment platform, and $500 into product or other necessary expenses, instead of spending $700 on a laptop, $200 on a website, and $100 on products. Knowing how to find the right balance and being willing to upgrade things, later on, ensures that you have everything you need to get started so that you can create the opportunity for you to upgrade in the future. If you start poorly, you may never create the funds or opportunities required to upgrade, which means that you have ultimately wasted your funds on poor investments.

Even as you begin to make more money and can upgrade to better tools, you must continue to hold onto the mindset of investing in only what is necessary for you to create your next opportunities. In doing this, you refrain from spending too much money on things that are unnecessary and instead keep that money available for other more important purchases. Which is, in fact, a major "secret" of the wealthy and elite. Although it may seem that they are living a lavish and luxurious lifestyle, most of the wealthy are incredibly focused on spending their money only on what matters and investing the rest elsewhere. Often, their investments into things like designer wardrobes are made purposefully so that they have a wardrobe that upholds their reputation and that will last. Both of which are necessary for saving or developing funds. Or, if you see them having expensive spa days or vacations, these are often the rewards they give themselves to help them stay relaxed and focused during the in-between times when they are focused on work and are essentially living with the bare basics. By knowing how and when to spend their money, wealthy people can easily create more wealth and maintain their wealth while also living a luxurious lifestyle.

Investing and Begin Creating Wealth

To make your financial future better than what it is today, there's only one thing that needs to happen. You need to start working hard to make it a reality. Money is going to be the key to a free life, but only if you start *doing* something about it right now. You don't need to be a financial whiz, a real estate savant or a savings expert to begin working on developing a smart strategy where you can begin investing your savings to create wealth. The only requirement you're going to need to bring to the table is your commitment and a strong desire for making it happen. This will take hard work.

When I was 16 years old, living in a foster home, I was on my way out the door only to see my foster dad, Leo, hard at work, sweating under the hot sun with slightly bleeding fingers. He was exhausted as he was carefully placing brick down on his driveway. I then looked at half of the driveway behind him, which had been already beautifully interlocked and said "Wow! Looks good Leo!". Out of the few years I lived in this home, I learned one thing, and its what he said to me next. He said, "Well if you want good things in life you got to work hard for it!". I have said that statement to myself, over and over again. Ever since the second, it left that man's mouth; I have made that statement as a part of my being!

If I said to you that it would be a piece of cake to take what your learning in this book and what you will learn in the coming chapters and apply it to your life to be easy and a quote-on-quote "Walk in the park" then I would be outright lying to you and doing you a disservice in helping you reach your financial freedom goals. For some of us, you are going to tweak a few things in your lifestyle to set yourself on the right track, but for others, like me when I was 16, you are going to be required to completely rearrange your entire life! No matter where you fall in this spectrum, your reading this book and a piece of you is still most likely in denial about your part of the deal, so let me put it in a coffin, nail it shut, and bury it 6 feet under for you; along with the other techniques and strategies which will be discussed in this chapter, this will require *commitment*, a *strong desire to execute*, and *hard work*!

Smart Ways to Begin Investing Your Money

When an investor is successful, it's not because they "just got lucky". You have been lied to if that's the case. What you are seeing is the *result* of a lot of careful planning and in-depth research that went into understanding the kind of investments they were getting themselves into, and how those investments aligned with the financial goals they set for themselves. Luck remained only a minor portion of the calculation. The challenge that most people face would be figuring out exactly how they should be investing their money, so they can effectively set themselves up for future success. While there certainly is no shortage of information and resources out there, the sheer volume of it can sometimes be more overwhelming than helpful.

Where Do Beginners Start?

When you think about investing your money, you're doing one of two things. You're either buying a certain portion of a company, or you're buying a commodity-based on the belief that the value of what you've just purchased is going to increase over time. This is not going to be another scheme to get rich overnight. This is a way to consistently build on the wealth that you've already got. Despite what you may figure, you needn't bother with a great deal of cash to begin. Even with the smallest amount, the compounding effect of the interest is what turns that small sum into a significant fortune with *time*. Provided that you choose the right investments of course.

While some people do successfully make their living by trading stocks, this is not the type of investing that most are going to benefit from. The surest way to benefit from your investment efforts is to do it long-term and let the money you've put in, compound over the next 10 or 20 years. That's how you're going to retire wealthier than you are now. The problem with short-term investments (trading in and out of the stocks you buy to make money quickly instead of holding onto those stocks for several years) is that while you can make your money this way, no matter how good you are or how exceptionally skilled you might be at trading, there will always be some amount of luck involved in the process. Even more so when you're just a beginner, and if you're not lucky, you could easily lose more than you profit.

Consider investing for long-term benefits. You will be able to minimize the risks involved and negate the occasional price-drops or short-term volatility that the market does experience now and then. Besides knowing how to pick the right kind of stocks, you're also going to need to be smart with your investments to reap the maximum profit. You don't have to be an intellectual genius or a financial whiz to achieve success, but you do need to know what the right moves the smart moves are to make:

Keeping It Real

Money may be the name of the game in investing, but it's not always about sticking your money into the stocks which are going to bring you the highest returns possible. Smart investing involves taking your investment objectives into careful consideration and then making realistic decisions that are going to lead you down the path towards reaching the financial goals you set for yourself at the beginning of this process. Think big picture and long-term.

Sticking to A Detailed Plan

The one urge you need to fight, especially when you're a beginner, is the urge that's going to tempt you to either sell or buy without first giving it some serious thought. Every investor needs to have a detailed plan. A plan that must be reviewed periodically to keep you focused on what you're trying to accomplish. Your plan needs to be as detailed and specific as possible, particularly when it involves your investment time frames and goals, the returns you need to make to reach your goals, what types of stocks or investments are going to be the best fit for your goals, and all the risks that you feel comfortable and confident enough to take to accomplish those goals. The plan could also include your plans for how you're going to diversify your investments.

Avoid Blind Trust

Keep yourself out of trouble and avoid blinding trusting anyone who comes along with a "good tip". Always, always, always do your due diligence and go the extra mile with your research. This is your money, what you worked so hard for, and what you're going to need to secure the free life you want. You must be confident and comfortable with every decision that gets made, and the smartest investment move you could make for yourself is to avoid blind faith and fairy tales. There is a simple rule of thumb that everyone should remember, regardless of whether you're investing or not. If something sounds far too good to be true, then it probably is. There are no confirmed promises, nor 100% guarantees when it comes to investment, and should anyone promise you as such, your red flag should always go up.

Never Borrow for Investments

As eager as you might be to begin your investment journey right away, never borrow to begin your investments. Borrowing is never a good idea, even more so when it comes to investments because should you lose your money or your investments don't pan out for some reason, you're going to be right back in debt again (or adding to your existing debt) when you owe someone money. The smartest thing to do would be to be patient, save and wait until you've got enough to begin investing with your own money. Using the 80/20 rule discussed in chapter 4 of this book you will be able to do this starting your last paycheck! Stop where you are in this book right now, log into your bank or reach into your pocket and set aside 20% from your last cheque before you continue reading the remaining chapters of this life-altering book.

Skip the Flip

Trying to outsmart or beat the market is where many investors stumble and fall. If you're a beginner, you should avoid stock flipping. Even if you're a seasoned investor you should try and stay away from it. Frequently selling and buying stocks is a proposition you will rarely win.

Protect Yourself from Common Investing Mistakes to Avoid

We all make mistakes along the way. Even the best investors out there have made mistakes along the way before they got to where they are. While mistakes are valuable life lessons in disguise, in the world of investments, they can be valuable life lessons that end up costing you a small fortune. To shield that from occurring, you have to secure yourself and your cash by dodging the most widely recognized errors that lead to a speculator's defeat.

Don't Get Impatient

Among the biggest causes of an investor's downfall is lacking patience. Recall the story of the hare and the tortoise? How slow and steady will always be the traits that win the race at the end of the day? Those lessons translate into everyday life too. In school, in your career, when you're exercising trying to lose weight, and of course, when it comes to investing. Pacing yourself and being patient are the qualities that will get you (and your money) further in the long run, your portfolio is not going to perform miracles overnight, and if that's what you were expecting when you started investing, you began for the wrong reasons.

Don't Invest in What You Don't Understand

Warren Buffett is arguably among the most recognized and successful investors in the world, and he has a sound piece of wisdom to impart to anyone who wants to go down this path. Never invest in what you don't understand. If you don't understand a company's business models, you should not be buying its stocks. This is one example of why diversified portfolios matter. Should you invest in individual stocks, you must understand what each stock represents for the business before you commit to investing. Otherwise, stick to mutual funds or exchange-traded funds until you find something up your alley.

Don't Get Attached

It's not personal, it's just business. You're buying a stock of a company to make money, and that's all it is. Getting too attached to the company can make you lose sight of why you invested in them, to begin with, and if any point the fundamentals that led to you investing with your chosen company change along the way, you should consider selling the stock (which can be hard to do if you get too attached to the company). Keep it neutral.

Don't Turnover Too Much

Jumping all over the place and in and out of your investments is going to kill your returns. The transaction costs are going to strip you of more money than you bargained for, and that's not even taking into account the short-term tax rates, along with all the long-term opportunities you miss for the really good investments.

Don't Wait to Get Back to Even

If you until a losing stock hopefully goes back to the original cost basis it started at before you sell it, you're potentially killing any chance of a profit you might have made. The stock that you're holding onto may continue sliding downwards until it becomes practically useless, which makes waiting until you get even again a mistake you should avoid.

Don't Let Emotions Rule You

When it comes to our finances, letting our emotions take over has never proved to be a good decision. Emotions lead to impulse buying (which leads to debt) and in investing, emotions lead to you losing out on your returns. Greed and fear are two toxic emotions that should always be avoided at all costs. Allowing them to slip into the decision-making process will prevent you from focusing on the bigger picture, make poor decisions in the heat of the moment and eventually end up costing you a lot of money.

Don't Ignore the Tax Consequence

The length that you hold onto your investments will be the one that influences your net worth ultimately. Your compounded annual earnings after your taxes are the one that matters in your investments. After-taxes is the keyword to focus on. Each time a portion of your earnings (in this case returns) gets taken away by Uncle Sam, that greatly diminishes the future value of the assets you've accumulated. Paying attention to the tax consequences and where you hold some of your assets could be helpful in significantly downsizing the payments you have to fork out. Keeping your municipal bonds which are tax-free in taxable brokerage accounts and holding your high dividend-yielding blue-chip stocks in a tax-free retirement account are some of the ways you could reduce your tax payments.

Don't Focus on Past Returns

Focusing too much on the past returns of an investment when you're choosing one to purchase is an investment mistake too. While you do need to look at how a particular fund performed when times were tough, it is important not to place too much emphasis on past performance. There could be several reasons why that fund performed poorly, but if what that fund lost was still markedly less than other similar funds during the same period, that could be an indication that the fund has a strong risk management system in place. Don't brush it off just yet, a fund's risk management measures are what's important at the end of the day.

Don't Rely on Recommendations Alone

The recommendation may have come from a friend, but there's no guarantee that it's necessarily a smart choice. These water cooler recommendations can be dangerous and trip you into jumping into buying those stocks without doing the proper due diligence just because "someone told you it was a good deal". Perhaps the stock did do well in the past, perhaps it didn't, but the more pertinent question you should be asking yourself is if it performed well in the past, is this performance going to be repeated? Will the following year's performance be as good as it was last year? The odds may not always be in your favor on that front.

Don't Hold Off on Harvesting Your Winnings

Your stock may have gone up, but that doesn't mean it is going to stay up forever. When your funds or stocks have risen to a point where you've made some substantial gains, the best move you can make would be to harvest some of your winnings.

Don't Invest Only Near the Top

To profit from your investment, you need to get in when the stocks are at their lowest and wait for it to rise again. Waiting on the sidelines until it's "safe" to rejoin the stock market could end up becoming a costly mistake since these "safe" periods usually mean the prices of these stocks have already risen by quite a substantial amount. Fear of seeing these market declines tend to hold a lot of investors back and to prevent yourself from making this mistake, you need to be the one that dictates the times when you buy and sell.

Investment Hacks to Make It Cooler

Another little piece of wisdom everyone can benefit from Warren Buffet is when he once said that you don't need to be a rocket scientist to invest. As complicated as the process may seem on the surface, but what's unfamiliar usually seems hard in the beginning until you get the hang of it.

If you want to give yourself your best chance of being wealthy, you need to do more than just earn money alone. You need to hold onto that extra money you brought in and find ways to make that money grow even more. One way of doing that, as you know by now, is through investments. Having several investments hacks up your sleeve certainly makes it easier too:

Starting Early

While it's never too late to get started, the earlier you start though the longer your money will have to grow over the long-term. You don't need to wait until you've accumulated a big sum before you begin. Every little bit matters when it comes to investing, even the smallest figure counts for something.

Keeping Tabs on Your Commissions and Fees

Funds that are being actively managed would naturally come with higher expense ratios than those of index funds. Keeping tabs on the fees and commission you're paying (if you're working with a broker) so you know exactly where your money is going. Try to have your fees the lowest as possible.

Don't Let Fear Hold You Back

Being afraid of the unknown is understandable. Investing in a possible unknown future can be scary to think about when you could potentially risk losing it all. However, if you're always going to wait for "the right time" or "until you become an expert", you're more likely to continuously put off ever getting started to begin with. Investments can be scary, but sometimes you need to take risks to make a change for the better. To ease your fears, perhaps consider starting with a smaller investment sum, to begin with, and increase that value as your confidence slowly grows along with it.

Make It a Little Celebration

Each time you accomplish an investment milestone, go ahead and celebrate your little victory as a reminder for yourself that patience and persistence will constantly win at the close of each day. Little victories like these are what keep you moving and keep you committed to staying on track, and it's okay to celebrate it by giving yourself or your family a little treat or two.

Picking Your Own Investments with Online Trading Platforms

If you're keen on becoming one of those do it yourself investors and you've already got some investment know-how, consider using online trading platforms to help you pick your investments. Let's say you've got $1,000 to invest, consider picking exchange-traded funds instead since they are better known for their diversification benefits and much lower costs.

Pre-Authorized Payment Plan

This is an agreement between a bank and an account holder whereby the account holder gives the bank permission to automatically debit the account by a specific amount and frequency. When I worked for one of the big 5 banks as one of their top Investment Sales Representatives, I would make sure that every one of my clients was set up with this Investment hack! Adding this hack to your investment strategy will decrease the average unit or share price; giving you more units/shares for less the investment. I'll explain how! For example, Scott and James both have the same Mutual Fund product with their bank. Scott set up a PPP for $100 that will come out of his account every Friday. James decided he will purchase units whenever he wants. Over the next four Fridays here is what happened with Scott's investment. The first Friday, the units cost $14.23, the second Friday each unit costs $14.78, the third Friday each unit costs $13.95, and the fourth Friday each unit costs $14.10. Scott had Pre-Authorized the bank to purchase $100 worth of units automatically on each of these days because he used the PPP method to set it and forget it. James on the other hand manually purchased $400.00 worth of units on the second Friday when the unit price was at $14.78. Both these individuals have the same mutual fund and both invested the same amount of money, however, Scott's average unit price turns out to be $14.25/unit over the 4 weeks and James average is $14.78 because he invested the entire $400 on the same day when the unit price was at $14.78. At the end of the month, Scott got more units than James for the same amount of money invested using this hack. Talk about a way to stretch your buck! Determine a fixed amount that will be scheduled to come out of your account every payday. Set up your PPP with your bank so that every payday that fixed amount gets taken out of your account and used to purchase units or shares in your investment products and watch your investments grow.

If You Need Help, Ask

Never feel afraid, embarrassed, or awkward to ask for help when you need it. If there's anything you're unsure of, it's always better to ask questions before you proceed any further. Better to be shy for a couple of minutes asking for help than to risk losing money because you were too shy to speak up. Investing can be an overwhelming process when you're new, and if at any point you're unsure, seek help from the experts. Brokerage firms, mutual funds, or exchange-traded funds have a customer service number you could ring up, and while they generally won't offer you any specific investment advice, they can point you in the right direction towards the tools which are going to help you make your decisions.

Creative Ways to Financial Freedom Think Outside the Box

The secret to becoming financially free is, well, no big secret at all. It's simply being able to exercise control over your finances, living below your means and avoid continually getting yourself into debt. Cutting back on how much you're spending is a fantastic first step in the right direction, but you know what's even better? Finding ways to add even more money to your bottom line. Not only is this finally going to put you within closer reach of your financial freedom goals, but more importantly, you'll be able to sustain this newfound freedom for the rest of your life.

I Have a Job, Why Should I Spend Time Making More Money?

The question is, why shouldn't you be jumping at a chance to make more money? That is what each of us wants at the end of the day. It's the reason why you have gotten this far in my book. You've got goals, dreams, things you would like to do, how you see yourself retiring one day. You're going to need money to make all that happen, and it's a simple case of the more you have, the better off you'll be. Money may not be the key to happiness because it is not, but it can certainly get you close enough to it. As money is not the most important thing in life, but at the end of the day, you still need it to survive comfortably in this world.

Why should you be spending your time making more money? Because it can help you do all the things in life which are important to you. Putting a roof over your family's head, securing your child's educational future, living out your retirement with financial security, leaving behind a financial legacy for your kids and grandkids to follow or inherit one day. Everyone wants to make money. Their reasons for doing so could be different, but the result is the same. It all boils down to getting more money.

Putting in the extra effort to earn more income can change your life. Besides becoming debt-free, you'll stop having to rely solely on your paycheck every month. You never have to worry again about not being able to afford the unexpected emergencies that come up now and then. You'll enjoy the thrill and the freedom of being able to make big purchases in cash (debt-free). Need more reasons as to why you should be finding ways to earn more money?

Because You Don't Want the Alternative

Try to imagine your life without a job and an income. Being broke all the time, wondering how you're going to make your next bill payments, not being able to do all the things you love. That's the alternative to not having money, and it's an alternative that you don't want. If you experienced job loss due to COVID-19, then you know what that is like as I write this book, I am doing it without a job and my non-essential business shut down.

Because You Don't Want to "Outlive" Money

Life may be short in other aspects, but not always when money is concerned. Once you hit retirement, you'll quickly realize how quickly your money disappears when it's not steadily coming in. Without proper financial planning, you'll most likely outlive your money and with a long way more to go in your retirement years, that's a situation you don't want to find yourself in. It's always better to have money in excess than to fall short.

Because You'll Never Be Short of It

Tired of always having to utter "I don't have enough money for this" or "I can't afford that"? Those complaints no longer have to be part of your life once you start earning more money. Provided you continue to live below your means of course because no matter what, if we are being honest with ourselves, the saying "enough, is never enough" is true to everyone to a certain degree and those who are starting on this path to financial freedom must foster contentment mixed with self-control to flush those complaints out of your vocabulary and way of life.

Because You Have the Time

If you've extra time that could be put towards earning you more money, why not do it? Everyone has 24 hours in their day, and the difference between those who've achieved financial success and those who haven't is how the former spends their time. They use their time wisely and productively, if there's an opportunity to make money, you can be sure they will not let it pass them by. How much time in your day do you have to invest in your financial future?

Because You're Doing This for Yourself

You're doing this for yourself, and maybe your family if you're married. You need to believe that you are worth investing in, that you are deserving of financial freedom, that you deserve a future where you're not constantly plagued by worrying thoughts about having a lack of money and debt that keeps piling up. You're doing this for yourself, and this short-term sacrifice is well worth it if it means securing your future.

Because You Could Retire Early

Many have dreams of early retirement, but because they feel stuck in their current financial situation, they don't see that as a possibility. Retiring early can happen if you put in the work now to make as much money as you can.

Because You'll Be Able to Follow Your Passion

Too many people allow their passion and their dreams to slowly die, resigning themselves to the fact that it's never going to happen with their current financial situation. Giving up is one of the worst mistakes you could make. "Follow your passion and experience your dreams" is only one of the numerous ways to keep us feeling cheerful and satisfied, regardless of whether it's venturing to the far corners of the planet, purchasing a vacation home, digging a well for clean water in parts of the earth where there is no access to clean drinking water, or starting a business of your own. If that's what you want for yourself one day, then that's all the motivation you need to get up and find ways to make more money. Write your goals, dreams, and passions down on paper and frequently go back to them and re-read why you are sacrificing and working hard in the area of your finances all over again and keep these fresh in your mind; you will be glad you did.

Because It's Freedom

For the very reason why you picked up this book in the first place. You need to achieve financial freedom for, all, of your life. Earning more money is how you create that freedom for yourself and your family.

Because It's Your Safety Net

Unemployment could strike at any time. You may have a secure job right now, but you never know when the situation may change, and taking for granted that you will have a steady paycheck to last you until retirement is how you let your guard down. A steady paycheck is good, but having that extra security and the safety net of even more income is going to protect you against possible unemployment. At least you'll still have a way of making some money until you land yourself another job again.

Because You'll Boost Your Savings

This one goes without saying, yet it's a reason that still gets overlooked when you're looking for reasons to persuade yourself to take on a little extra work for more money. Let your savings account and the excitement of seeing that number gradually increase be your reason.

Because You Can Afford to Take Risks

Making more money is going to help out your investment efforts. When you've got cash to spare, you're able to take more calculated risks with your investments without going into debt or jeopardizing your existing savings, and never have to miss out on an opportunity because you didn't have enough funds for it.

Ways to Make More Money

Having a side hustle means you don't have to depend on your employer any longer for your next raise. Part of being financially free is taking control of your finances. You're the one that gets to say how much money you're making and spending each month. Your income is now determined by how much you work, rather than being dictated by an employer. How you could earn an extra income are unlimited, with the only limit being how much or how *hard* you're willing to work to put in the hours. We're fortunate to be living in a digital world, where endless possibilities are abundant, many of which weren't available several decades or even years ago. Making extra money now might not even require you to leave the comfort of your home, and all you need is a computer, the time and a good internet connection to get you going. Consider these out of the box thinking possibilities which you could turn to for those extra dollars:

Become A Search Engine Evaluator

Who would have thought that this could be a real gig that you get paid for? Search engine evaluators rely on search engines that are used the most frequently and seek out possible errors or bugs in the system. It may not pay a lot, but it's a gig you don't have to leave the couch for at least.

Be an Etsy Store Owner

Hone your creative talents or skills and put them to good use by becoming an Etsy store owner. If your passion for creating art, making DIY keepsakes, or even creating unique pieces of clothing could be used to generate an income, you're sitting on an untapped opportunity.

Get Paid for Completing Surveys

It's a slow-moving way to make some extra income, but if you've got some time to spare and you don't mind answering a couple of questions, you might as well get paid for your time and complete some surveys while binge-watching your favorite TV shows or movies.

Start Affiliate Marketing

Spending too much time on social media could have its uses after all, and if you've got a large following, there might be an opportunity to parlay your connections and turn that into cash with the right affiliate marketing strategies.

Becoming a Social Media Manager

Once again, put your love for social media to good use by using your skills and knowledge of how these platforms work by offering your services as a social media manager. Busy companies could be on the lookout for services just like yours.

Becoming a Blogger

If you're starting a blog for the sole purpose of making money though, you're starting it for the wrong reasons. Starting your blog is suitable for those who have a specific niche topic that they're knowledgeable and passionate about. Combined with a flair for stringing sentences together, you can share your knowledge with the world and when you're good at what you do, only then will the money follow.

Become a Published Author

The same principle as becoming a blogger, this one works best if you've got a topic you're passionate about and a flair for writing to boot. Becoming a self-published author is so easy these days, thanks to the magic and wonder of Amazon with no upfront financial investment required to get started.

Be A Freelance Editor or Writer

Another way you could put your writing skills to good use would be to become a freelance editor or writer. There's no shortage of work with this one, especially online with job openings constantly available on sites like Fiverr, Upwork, and a myriad of other options to choose from. Once again, technology has made working remotely from anywhere you are a fantastic opportunity to earn some extra income every month.

Becoming a YouTuber

Think to blog, except this time on video (that's why they call it blogging). The same rules still apply, you need a specific topic or niche area that you're passionate about, except this time instead of writing, the other requirement that's needed is the time to create, film and edit videos regularly. You're also going to have to be comfortable and natural in front of the camera. Love what you do and the money (and followers) will start rolling in.

Buying and Selling Domain Names

Similar to real estate flipping, except you're doing it online with domain names instead. If you've got a knack for sourcing popular domain names that have yet to be discovered, there's a good opportunity to make some money by buying and then reselling those websites. Domain names are available for as little as $2.99 on websites like GoDaddy.com for example, but there could be ones that cost a little more. Once you've found the one you like, purchase and then market that domain name on Flippa.com for a higher flat-rate. It's that simple!

Be A Virtual Assistant

Your organizational skills might just be your ticket to earning extra cash on the side. Virtual assistants would do what any other assistants do. Respond to their clients' emails, schedule work, post content, prepare proposals and mock-up letters, even perform data entry work. Easy enough work, considering you get to do all of this remotely.

Be an Online Translator

Thank you once again, to the internet, who has opened so many doors and incredible new opportunities. Now, even being bilingual can be turned into a money-making opportunity. Depending on the skill-set that you're offering, you could find work transcribing recordings of lessons or speeches, providing translation services through Skype, or even find work doing translations for eBooks and blog content.

Work in Customer Service Remotely

If you've got the patience and a love for helping others, working remotely in a call center could be right up your extra income alley.

Renting on Airbnb

Do you live alone with an extra room to spare? Don't mind the prospect of having the occasional stranger in your home now and then? Is your home located in an excellent part of town, close to plenty of public transportation and basic amenities? Your spare room could be generating some income for you if you list it on Airbnb.

Tutoring Online

Patience and a love for teaching others could mean money in the bank when you sign up to become an online tutor for those who are seeking out services just like yours. There's even a market for teaching English online too where you could easily make up to $22 an hour.

Becoming a TaskRabbit-er

Get connected with other locals who need help now and then completing their chores or errands and get paid for it by signing up on TaskRabbit.com. Some people enjoy the variety of being able to take on different tasks now and then, if that is you then create extra income for yourself and what you love.

Becoming A Lyft or Uber Driver

Some love driving more than others, and if you're the former with a vehicle that's reliable, driving around in your spare time could now translate to money in the bank. Even more so during peak travel hours when both demand and fares are higher. Uber has even expanded to Uber Eats, and instead of picking up customers, you're delivering food to nearby locations in your area.

Babysitting in Your Spare Time

Love being around kids? There's always a market for good, reliable babysitters.

Selling Your Pictures

Anyone with an eye for creative detail and a good camera can now sell their photographs online and generate a pretty good passive income stream if you're good at what you do.

Activity: Apply What You Learned

1. Pick your top 5 favorite ways of creating wealth listed above and do a 30 minutes search on each of your top 5 and answer these questions:

   - What is the total startup cost to begin?
   - How much time/day will this require of me?
   - What obstacles are currently in the way that is hindering me from starting to make money using this platform right now?

2. What do I need to do right now to remove or solve those obstacles and start today?

3. From your top 5, now pick your top 3 from that list. Over the next 72 hours commit to starting making money using these 3 platforms. Once the dust settles; I would encourage you to add

the remaining 2 from your list so you have 5 different streams of income!

Starting Your Own Business Avoid Common Pitfalls

What if your passion and dreams involve starting a business of your own? That's an incredible goal to have, there's nothing more empowering than starting something you love from scratch, putting all your blood, sweat, and tears into it to finally watch it blossom and grow into something successful. Being your own boss does come with its ups and downs, but for those who love what they do, every day is another day that's worth it if it means they get to do what they love.

One of the biggest risks that follow the entrepreneurship path is the danger of making mistakes which could end up costing you not just your money, but your business entirely. Many businesses have had to shut down operations due to poor decisions that ended up being too costly to bounce back from. However, whenever you're beginning something new, you're bound to make mistakes along the way, it's not entirely avoidable. Making mistakes along the way is part of the learning process, but you don't want to make too many mistakes that are going to end up costing you a lot of money down the road.

If you know someone who's a successful business owner, they could prove to be a great source of information. Even better if they're willing to be your mentor during the crucial early stages of your business when every decision you make matters. Alternatively, you could turn towards the advice listed below for some words of wisdom, and avoid these common pitfalls which might lead to your downfall.

Never Be Afraid to Fail

It feels like an almost impossible request, but this is one of the biggest mistakes to be made. If you're far too afraid to fail, then perhaps entrepreneurship might not be the most suitable path for you to follow. Business is risky, challenges are numerous, but ultimately it is how you rise again and learn from your failures that will be the key to your success.

Be Organized

There's no upper management or senior supervisor to tell you what to do anymore. You are now going to run the show from start to finish, failure to organize and prioritize is how your business will slip through your fingers.

Moving Far Too Slowly

Being afraid of making mistakes and moving far too slow with your business decisions is just as bad as making rushed decisions. You shouldn't move too quickly, but neither should you move too slowly. Coming to the realization too slowly that your business relationship isn't working, or that your customer is not willing to pay the asking price, or even being too slow to recognize that investors are losing interest could end up costing you your business.

Never Skip Your Due Diligence

Due diligence matters not just in finding the right investments for your financial portfolio, but for the business decisions, you make too. Doing your research will keep you from misinterpreting your market. To avoid overestimating or underestimating your costs, misreading the market demand, or appealing to an entirely wrong demographic, never skip the due diligence, or you'll be killing your business before it's even had a chance to begin. This is where a S.W.O.T. analysis could be helpful. Find out what the Strengths, Weaknesses, Opportunities, and Threats are for the business you would like to start and decide if your business decision is feasible or not.

Rushing the Hiring Process

When you've got your business all set up, you're now eager to fill it with employees and get things going. Unfortunately, as a start-up, rushing the hiring process can prove detrimental to your business. Hiring full-timers instead of part-timers which might make more sense is one example of poor decisions that get made without thinking them through. Hiring employees costs money, whether your business is making a profit or not, and you need to gauge your needs accurately and avoid rushing the hiring process.

Always Have Contracts in Place

Even with suppliers with whom you've got a solid working relationship. A business should never be mixed in with your personal life, and no matter how good of a relationship you have, it can quickly come to an abrupt halt if there are no black and white agreements available. Strong documentation must become a way of life in business, as this will always provide something to revert to when things get hot between you and your employees, Landlord, suppliers, or other individuals that you do business with because in one way or another — they will — get hot — at least once!

No Business Plan

A major misstep is to go into business without one. A business plan is like the foundation of your home, without a foundation, your house will not be able to stand for long. Without a business plan as your business' foundation, it's only a matter of time before that comes tumbling down. As crucial as this is to start a successful business you should not spend to much time putting this together or else you may suffer a state of analysis paralysis. I want you to avoid this pitfall, so if you spend more then 20 minutes putting together your initial business model with this tool, then you are doing it wrong! The Lean Canvas business model tool is easy, puts your entire initial business model on one page, and did I mention that it will only take you 20 minutes?!

Paying Yourself the Wrong Amount

It's not always easy to decide how much salary you should give yourself as the owner of the business. It's much easier to determine the salary of an employee than it is to decide on your own. To avoid overpaying or underpaying yourself, consider making your salary a percentage of the revenue that gets made.

Asking for Too Much Advice

Understandably, you're eager to get as much advice as possible from various sources if you can, since you don't want to make mistakes. However, asking too many different people for suggestions and advice could be a case of "too many cooks spoil the broth". Every person you ask is going to have their advice on how to go about doing things, but at the end of the day, it is you who has to make the ultimate decision. Have an advisory board consisting of a select few individuals whose advice you trust and that will have to do.

Not Focusing on Sales Enough

Sales and product development are among the two major driving forces of your business, and while focusing on product development is important since you need products to get the sales going, you could put yourself at risk of spending too much time on the former that you risk neglecting the sales aspect of it. You need a great product to build a great company, but spending too much time in product development puts you at risk of losing customers to your competitors. Launch your product and use client feedback to make it better as you go, but don't forget to thank your clients for their feedback, even giving them a discount on their next purchase can go a long way. Many of the wealthiest people on earth who have big well-known corporations like Bill Gates from Microsoft have built their business from client feedback! That is, negative, client feedback! Good feedback is a great encouragement, but, negative feedback is even better encouragement for the successful entrepreneur. It is used to grow its establishment and improve how they do business. Feedback also improves the services offered to the public.

Not Having Enough Capital

Getting the funds needed to buy equipment, rent an office space and stock inventory is only the beginning, and raising enough capital to only cover those basics is another mistake that gets many by many new businesses. You need to have enough capital to sustain not just your rent and equipment, but your employees' salaries, insurance, overhead expenses, utilities, and other miscellaneous expenses required, and you're going to need enough capital to sustain you until your business can turn a profit. Before you even begin to open the doors to your business, work on calculating exactly how much capital you need to raise for the foreseeable future.

Conclusion

There is no overnight solution to financial freedom; at the same time, it is not like there is no open way to any solution. Ways and methods as discussed in this book are available, and we end this book by cheering such individuals who believe in the term, 'change is possible' and can be better than before, by dedicating it to them.

Having a plan that you can immediately refer back to will be one of the better things that you can accomplish, in terms of helping yourself be ready for whatever financial hits come your way in life; should that time arrive, you have to be able to stand on your own two feet. Being independent on your own will be one of the biggest things that you can do in terms of taking charge of your financial situation.

Going above and beyond in your preparations at the beginning of your journey to financial freedom may seem a little excessive. In the long run, you will be happy that you made this decision as you will have the safety and security, that if the bottom falls out of your financial plans, that you will be able to take comfort in the fact that you have a little extra money set aside and are ready to suffer through what can, at times, be a tough financial dry spell. If you know where you can trim some of the excess spending, then you will have a battle plan in place that allows for you to continue where you left off when the bottom falls out of your economic plans.

Finally, I cannot say this enough: taking the principals, lessons, and recommendations that you learned in this book and applying them to your life from now onward will deliver you an ROI where the sky will not be the limit because you will have the stars to land on.

Dear Reader;

I am delighted that you have read my book and I trust that it has empowered you to take control of your finances and opened your horizon to a brighter financial future for you and your children's children!

I would appreciate it if you would be so kind to leave me a positive review.

Within your review you can quote your favorite part too if you wanted because along with myself, others would appreciate finding out how my book helped you!

Many thanks once again.

Angelo Shamoon